Uncovering Northampton's Past

Author Adrian H Perkins

Researchers

Tina Cockerill

Mark Marriott

Adrian H Perkins

Published by New Generation Publishing in 2024

Copyright © Adrian Perkins 2024

First Edition

ISBN: 978-1-83563-410-3

www.newgeneration-publishing.com

New Generation Publishing

Acknowledgements

Richard Blacklee

Judy Cooper

Northampton & County Club

Northamptonshire Archives Service

The National Archives, London.

The Pontifical Institute for Medieval Studies collection, held in the University of Toronto Library

Northamptonshire Archaeological Society
Andy Chapman BSc MCIfA FSA
1975 Trench observations W R G Moore and B Giggins.

Reference books.

With kind permission from the following.
Whellan's Directory of Northamptonshire 1849
www.my-history.co.uk

A History of the Church of All Saints, Northampton by Serjeantson, Robert Meyricke, 1861- Publication date 1901.
The Pontifical Institute for Medieval Studies collection, held in the University of Toronto Library

Introduction

I have lived in Northampton all my life and watched the town progress through its many changes. We all know change has to happen and there is no stopping it. However, the loss of many iconic buildings over the years has taken away much of the town's identity and character.

Northampton was once the most important town in the country. Kings and queens held parliament meetings here and set off to the Crusades. It was at Northampton that one of the most successful of the Crusades was inaugurated. In 1239, Richard, Earl of Cornwall (brother of Henry III.) and many other barons who had taken the cross, assembled here, and went to the church of All Saints where they bound themselves by an oath, sworn upon the high altar, to conduct their troops direct to Palestine, and not to engage in any other warfare on the way.

That is just one example of how important this town was. Now we only have a handful of historic buildings to tempt the history-loving visitors to our town. Most buildings are post-1675, apart from some superb churches and some hidden gems from the mid-14th century. These hidden gems must be brought out into the public gaze, something to be cherished and shared with others. Our heritage could bring visitors to this town, but only if we look after it, study it, and bring the information to the wider audience. This booklet was done for just that reason.

The search for early buildings and their owners/tenants in George Row pre-fire of Northampton, 1675, is extremely difficult the further back you search. However, with the help of my friends, Tina Cockerill and Mark Marriott, we have had some success. Names and places are from that period in time and do not always follow today's spelling.

We hope you find our research interesting.

Research of tenements in streets around All Saints Church in the Centre of Northampton, with particular reference to the medieval undercroft and cellars in George Row

Our initial objective in writing this booklet was to take the history of the rib-vaulted cellars below the Northampton and County Club in George Row back as far as possible. Who owned the land and why was the cellar built, we thought that would be our final destination. However, searching the archives of Northampton and the National archives in London took us on a journey of discovery that we felt compelled to follow. Our passion for early Northampton history took over and below you can read our findings. We hope the information and references given will help others to take the search even further.

The first and most important thing to remember when searching for the street known as George Row is that we could find no early documentation with that name on until the 17 century. Before that date, it was called Spicers Row, or {le Spicersrow}. We found several references to Spicers Row to the south of All Saints Church in the Northampton and National archives.

In this document we endeavoured to give factual evidence instead of guesswork. People have surmised, and we have seen quotes, that the cellars/undercroft below the Northampton and County Club building were at some point in time a subterranean chapel. Indeed, if you look at the architecture, thought to date from the early to mid-14th century, there was certainly a great deal of money spent on its construction. Power and wealth at that time in Northampton were in the hands of land-owning knights and various religious institutions. With the proximity of All Saints church to the north, we can see why the cellars are thought to have ecclesiastical beginnings. But is that true?

Our task was to research its very earliest beginning so with that in mind we needed to start with All Saints Church and find its earliest possible records. Because of its proximity were they once joined?

Now let us go back to around 1066 and the Norman conquest of Britain. Contrary to popular belief the conquest was spread over many years with King William spending the vast majority of his time in France, leaving control of England in the hands of his half-brother Odo and one of his closest supporters, William Fitz Osbern. King William was not secure on the English throne until after 1072.

William systematically dispossessed English landowners and conferred their property on his continental followers. Simon de St. Liz (Senlis), accompanied William "the Conqueror" to England. He was created Earl of Huntingdon and Northampton in [1087/90]. Sometime in the period 1093–1100, he and his wife, Maud, founded the Priory of St Andrew's, As well as the Holy Sepulchre church in Northampton, he also built Northampton Castle and the town walls.

The Language of old English now gained Norman French words, they slowly entered the English language, and the usage of names common in France instead of Anglo-Saxon names soon became common. Male names such as William, Robert, and Richard became widespread.

It is important for you to understand the way Northampton, and some of its buildings were affected during the years of transition from Saxon to Norman times.

The following information shows the transition of All Saints church into the Norman era.

Ref: A history of the Church of All Saints, Northampton by Serjeantson, Robert Meyricke, 1861
Publication date 1901
Topics All Saints' Church (Northampton, England), genealogy
Publisher Northampton, W. Mark
Northampton possessed several churches of a quasi-parochial character a century or two before the Norman Conquest; nor need there be much doubt that the central one of All Saints occupied a portion of the site of the present fabric.

The town was burnt by the Danes in 1010. It was speedily rebuilt, but again to a great extent laid waste by fire and sword in 1064. Recovery from this last calamity was slow, for at the time of the Domesday Survey (1087) many of the houses were still in a ruinous condition and uninhabited. The survey mentions under the royal lands that " The King has in the demesne of Portland, two carucates, (a medieval unit of land area nominally regarded as an area of 120 acres) and two parts of a third carucate and twelve acres of meadow. One carucate of land belongs to the church of St. Peter and half a carucate to the church of All Saints." This is the first historic mention of the church. Indeed, this Domesday passage does not expressly state that these two churches belonged to Northampton; it is also true that the survey mentions churches dedicated both to St. Peter and to All Saints at Aldwincle and at Rushton, but the statement in the same passage as to " nine pounds and " twelve shillings for other issues of the town " cannot apply to either of these two villages. Portland probably lay to the south of the town in Far Cotton, where an Elizabethan survey of the townlands mentions Port Lane as a boundary of the Moor Field pertaining to Cotton.

There is evidence in the fabrics themselves of two of the Northampton churches (St. Sepulchre's and St. Peter's) of pre-Norman work. Unfortunately there is nothing of the kind that has as yet been discovered about the stones of All Saints, but the intelligent student of our local history will be troubled with no doubts as to the original existence of a Saxon church under the name of All Saints, Northampton. The earliest known charter conferred by Simon de St. Liz (Senlis) and Maud his wife on the Priory of St. Andrew, grants, among other numerous gifts of lands and churches, the church in which they worship, and all other churches of the town with their appurtenances. The witnesses to this undated charter, though numerous, do not enable us to ascertain the year with exact precision, but it was at all events before 1090 and not earlier than 1084. A confirmatory charter dated 1108 is an imposing document on account of the high position of most of the witnesses who included amongst their number, King Henry, Queen Matilda, David of Scotland, Archbishop Anselm, and the Bishops of Lincoln, Chester, Rochester, and London. In this case, the church of All Saints is specifically mentioned as evidently being the most important Christian fabric of the town outside the walls of the Priory. It is the only church to which a name is assigned. The actual words of the charter are, Ipsam ecclesiam omnium Sanctorum, et omnes ejusdem mile ecclesias.

It may, we think, with reasonable probability, be conjectured that the old Saxon church of All Saints, damaged considerably in the onslaughts on the town burned by Thorkil's Danes in 1010 and again facing ravages in 1064, would be rebuilt by the Earl of Northampton and the inhabitants, after the Norman fashion, before its formal transference to the Priory of St. Andrew. The original size of All Saints Church was considerably larger than what we see today, its boundaries went further North, South, East, and West. Unfortunately no sketches pre-1600 are available of how the church once looked, however, John Speed's map of the town centre dated 1610 seems to be the most accurate, although we have seen conflicting sketches of the church drawn pre-fire of 1675.

In 1975 the GPO and the Water Board dug trenches around Northampton Town Centre. Northamptonshire Archaeological Society was allowed to observe and take detailed notes on what was found in these trenches. What follows are their observations. I added these notes to give the reader a sense of timescale, it also provides an idea of the original depth of the medieval levels. While looking at underground medieval structures leading out into streets, original street levels must always be taken into consideration.

For your reference, while reading the notes below a metalled road is also known as a paved road, and SP with numbers after them are grid reference numbers.

GPO TRENCHES

Derngate (June-July 1975). The GPO trench ran along Derngate, N. of the medieval road. It went through several cellars of post-medieval date built of stone and brick (e.g. SP 75636044, SP 75726038).

Derngate (SP 75686041). A large pit about 4.25m. diameter, up to 1.57m. deep, it contained several 16th century sherds including a near-complete Frechen stoneware jug, many animal bones, and shells (oyster, cockle and mussel).

Derngate (SP 75806034). July 1975. Walls and foundations of building(s) along 14m. of the trench at 0.50 — 1.60m. depth. One foundation of fine ashlar and floors of clay and earth were seen. The date is probably medieval or early post-medieval. Several tile fragments, a few medieval sherds and one late Roman sherd were found.

Derngate (SP 75896029). In June 1975 a substantial wall foundation, 2.54m. deep at the lowest point, running N.E./S.W. with a clay floor adjoining on the S.E. side at a depth of 1.60m.

6

Derngate (SP 75916029). June-July 1975. A roughly constructed sandstone wall, running N.E./ S.W. at the junction with Spring Gardens proved to be part of a post-medieval cellar.

Derngate (SP 75916029). In June 1975 a fairly large pit containing several 15th-i 6th century sherds, oyster and mussel shells and a few animal bones.

Derngate (SP 75926029). In July 1975 a small deposit of medieval painted window glass was found with a few 16th century sherds.

Derngate (SP 75926028). July 1975. A very large excavated feature up to 2.30 m. deep, either a pit or possibly a terminal of the medieval defensive ditch, it contained a number of medieval and later finds. These finds included several sherds of c. 14th to 16th century date, several tile fragments, animal bones, oyster and mussel shells.

George Row July-August 1975. A series of soil and stone layers and at least one metalled road level were found. Natural at the E. end (SP 75506044) found at 1.02m. and at the W. end (SF 75406042) at a depth of 1.68m. The few finds include leather offcuts, medieval sherds and animal bones.

George Row (SP 75486043), July 1975. A small feature, possibly a pit or ditch, up to 1.80m. below the road surface, contained several early medieval sherds and a few animal bones.

George Row (SP 75466043). In August 1975 an E./W. foundation of large sandstone blocks, 0.40m below the road surface and c. 4m. S. of All Saints is the 19th century and earlier churchyard wall.

George Row (SP 75436042). In August 1975, formerly within the churchyard, at least ten inhumations were found at depths between 0.75 — 1.75m., one in a well-made stone cist with mortared stones at a maximum depth of 1.31 m. Two other burials were in poorly made cists. A short length of E./W. wall, 2m South of All Saints (SF75446042), was also recorded.

Bridge Street (SP 75386041). In September 1975 a series of four metalled road levels of packed sandstone fragments and clay layers were found to a depth of 1.45m., the trench bottom. Finds include a few medieval sherds, leather fragments and iron slag.

Gold Street (SP 75376042). In September 1975 a layer of black and grey clay containing organic material recorded from a depth of 1.75m. to the trench bottom at 2.10m. Several early medieval sherds, leather fragments including part of a shoe, several animal bones and wood fragments were found.

Drapery. September — November 1975. A succession of metalled roads, stone, sand, and soil layers. At the S. end (SP 75406042) two road levels were found, the lower at a depth of 1.78m. resting on natural. At the N. end (SF 75396056) one road level was found at 0.63m. resting on natural. In the central area however (SP 75406052), four or five road levels were identified, the lowest at 1.74m, on natural. Several medieval sherds, leather offcuts (In the central and S. part of the Street), and a few animal bones were found.

Drapery. In November 1975 finds of organic material were made in the S. half of the Drapery preserved in layers of black and grey clay at depths between 0.48 — 1.70m. The main concentration of finds occurred outside No. 21-23 (SF 75406051) with a lesser concentration outside No. 15-17 (SF 75406049). Many leather offcuts and fragments were found including a few shoe soles and knife sheaths, wood fragments, two bone points, several animal bones and a few medieval sherds.

Drapery (SP 75376061). In December 1975 a wall foundation was visible at a depth of 1.00 — 1.80m Loose soil fill adjacent contained burnt material and a few post-medieval objects

As we can see from the descriptions, it is very important to remember the original road depth. Especially when investigating mid 14th century cellars with, what were once windows looking out to the street, are now simply pavement lights.

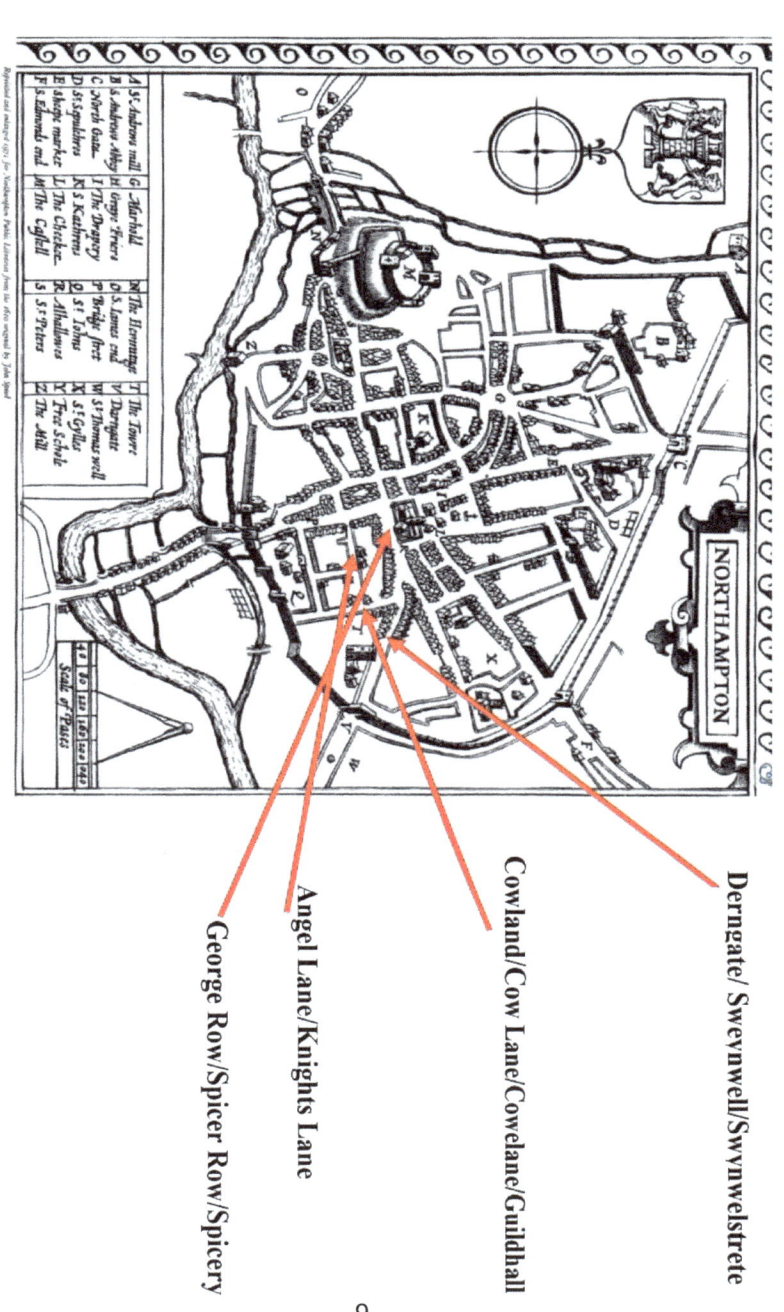

John Speed's map of the town entre in 1610. Tina Cockerill has added the medeival street names to the map for your referance.

Derngate/ Sweynwell/Swynwelstrete

Cowland/Cow Lane/Cowelane/Guildhall

Angel Lane/Knights Lane

George Row/Spicer Row/Spicery

9

Whellan's Directory of Northamptonshire 1849
www.my-history.co.uk
P119

Crypts.

Besides the portion of the ancient crypt beneath the chancel of All Saints Church, there is a portion of another crypt a little to the south of it, under the residence of H. B. Whitworth, Esq. George-row, which is supposed to have had a passage, now stopped up, to the former.

At the southwest end of College Street, groined arches still remain in some cellars. It has been supposed that this was the site of All Saints' College, from which this lane, recently (as in many other instances,) promoted to the rank of a street, derived its appellation, and in the drapery beneath the house of Mr. Wetton is another crypt with groined arches of decorated architecture. There is also a corbel, consisting of a face, with the tongue lolling out; and it is impossible to ascertain the establishment to which this crypt belonged. There is also here, an ainbre locker, which no doubt formed a part of the usual arrangement of a chapel to some religious foundation

The Northampton & County Club Vaulted Cellars

At this point, I would like to insert a map of the cellar/undercroft in George Row. The map took us a couple of months to produce. We identified different stages of the building work over the centuries, these differences are colour-coded. This will be followed by photographs identifying each room and our findings within those rooms. The passage mentioned in connection to the Whitworth Chambers in the article on crypts above is room (J) on the following map.

A larger version of this map is available to view in the history reference section of Northampton Central Library in Abington Street.

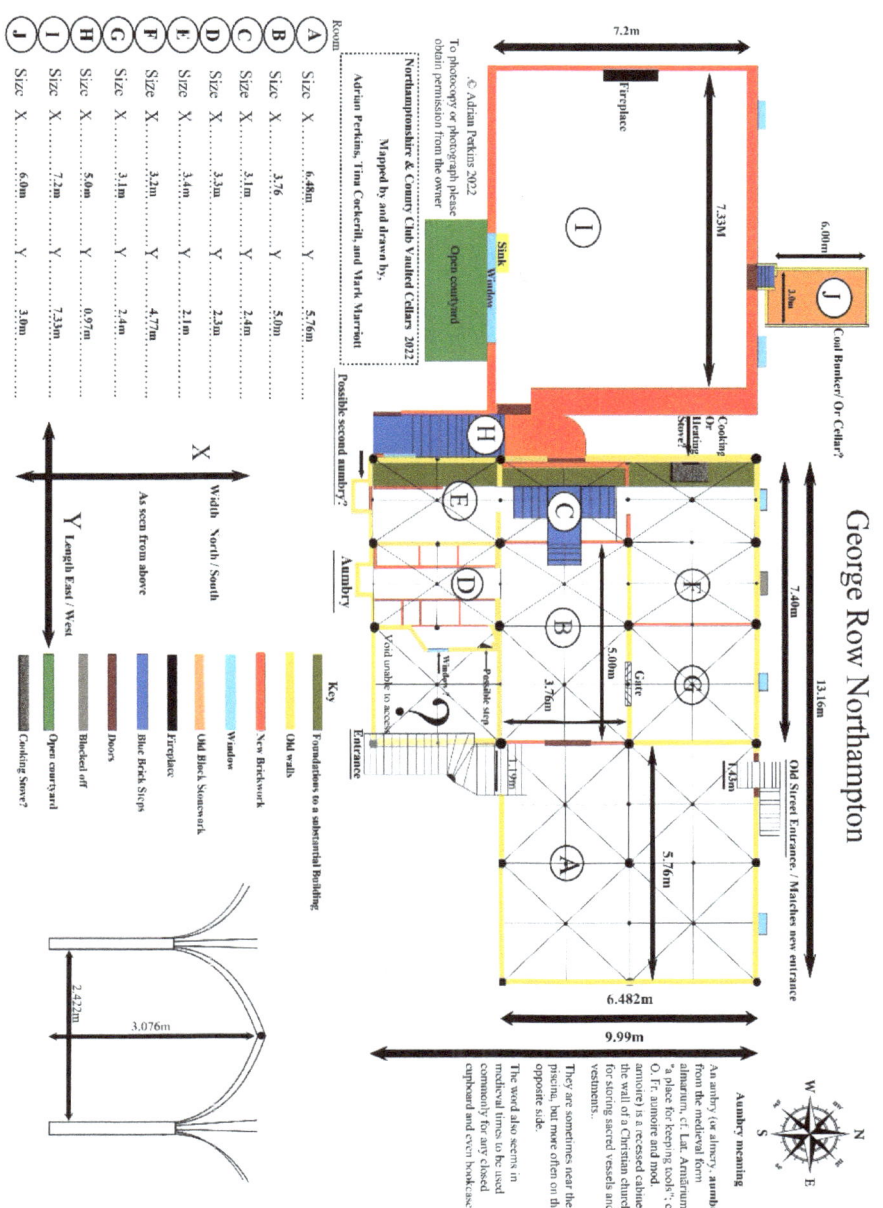

George Row Northampton

Northamptonshire & County Club Vaulted Cellars 2022

Mapped by, and drawn by,
Adrian Perkins, Tina Cockerill, and Mark Marriott

© Adrian Perkins 2022

To photograph or photograph please obtain permission from the owner

Room		Size	X		Y	
A	Size	X	6.48m	Y	5.76m
B	Size	X	3.76	Y	5.0m
C	Size	X	3.1m	Y	2.4m
D	Size	X	3.3m	Y	2.3m
E	Size	X	3.4m	Y	2.1m
F	Size	X	3.2m	Y	4.77m
G	Size	X	3.1m	Y	2.4m
H	Size	X	5.9m	Y	0.97m
I	Size	X	7.2m	Y	7.33m
J	Size	X	6.0m	Y	3.0m

X — Width North / South — As seen from above

Y — Length East / West

Key

Foundations to a substantial Building
Old walls
New Brickwork
Window
Old Black Stonework
Fireplace
Black Steps
Blue Brick Steps
Doors
Blocked off
Open courtyard
Cooking Stove?

Aumbry meaning

An aumbry (or almery, aumbry; from the medieval form almarium, cf. Lat. Armārium, O. Fr. aumoire and mod. "a place for keeping tools"; cf. aumoire) is a recessed cabinet in the wall of a Christian church for storing sacred vessels and vestments.

They are sometimes near the piscina, but more often on the opposite side.

The word also seems in medieval times to be used commonly for any closed cupboard and even bookcase.

Possible second aumbry?

Aumbry

Entrance

Old Street Entrance / Matches new entrance

The photo above shows the entrance steps leading down into the first cellar room

The photo below shows the bottom of the staircase.

The photo above gives an idea of the descent into the cellar.

Room (A) on the map. Note the hexagonal columns have no visible base. Maybe the original floor level and column bases remain buried below.

The photo above shows room (A) on the map and the original entrance from the street South of All Saints Church. An interesting point to note is the modern-day entrance is directly above and in line with the medieval one. Traces of iron hinges can still be seen embedded in the walls.

Room (B) on the map with rooms left and right. Note the blue machinery bricks, possibly from the 1940s. The cellars were used as an air raid shelter during WW2.

Room (D) on the map. On the back wall is what is believed to be an original Ambry.

An ambry (or almery, aumbry; from the medieval form almarium, cf. Lat. Armārium, "a place for keeping tools"; cf. O. Fr. aumoire and mod. armoire) is a recessed cabinet in the wall of a Christian church for storing sacred vessels and vestments. They are sometimes near the piscina, (In the context of Catholic and pre-Reformation churches, a piscina refers to a stone basin located near the altar) but more often on the opposite side. The word also seems in medieval times to be used commonly for any closed cupboard and even bookcase. The later brickwork you can see covers hinges to the right of the cupboard rendering it useless.

This photo shows the east wall of room (D). High up you can see what looks like a window, or opening, cut into the stonework.

Room (G) on the map. A coal shoot seems to have been cut into the north wall out to the street. A window may have existed at some time, it would have been symmetrical within the archway, as in the photo on the following page

This photo shows the entrance to the west end of room (F), as seen from the landing in room (C).

Room (F) on the map. This shows what is thought to be a bricked up window in the north wall out to the street. Notice the wear at its base. Room (F) is double the length of room (G).

The photo to the left shows the west wall of room, (F) just inside the door.

There are remnants of an iron stove or boiler with a square hole above for a chimney pipe. Could this be from the time of the infirmary? Maybe an early heating system?

This photo shows room (E) as seen from room, (C) on the map. Room
(C) is just a landing above the blue brick steps we saw earlier. Note
the masonry covering almost half of the width of room (E). It
continues into room (F).

We also found another bricked up cupboard or doorway on the south wall. The original floor in this room would have been much lower than today. That goes for the entire complex.

The cellars now extend to the west through a passage, (H) on the map, and under a building known as Whitworth Chambers. The walls between the previous cellars and the Whitworth cellars are some six feet thick.

The photo above shows room (I) on the map. The cellar below Whitworth Chambers. In the photo you are looking north out to George Row and the door to room (J) is just to the left of the skylight

The photo above shows room (J) on the map, a barrel-vaulted cellar running six meters north out below the street from the Whitworth Chambers.

1215: William Tilly (1st recorded mayor of Northampton)

1300s

Cellared buildings were constructed on Spicers Row, The Drapery, and the Southwest end of College Street, suggesting there was a high demand for land in central areas even after the population had started to decline.

We know that Spicers Row was to the South of All Saints Church with tenements bequeathed to The Prior and Convent of St Andrews, next to the tenement of Henry Spicer. The Drapery was, and is to this day, on the west side of the church.

The cellars we are investigating are thought by some to be unfinished. As we know, they were built in the early to mid-14th century, so what happened next may give answers to why they seem unfinished.

The Plague of 1349

The plague was raging in Northamptonshire from May to October 1349 and was at its worst in the county in August. The town itself seems to have been attacked most severely in October. Of the beneficed clergy of the county, 146 died out of a total of 281, but the proportion would be far larger amongst the unbeneficed, especially those who were monks and friars. At this time, out of the nine beneficed clergy of Northampton six died, the Vicars of St. Mary, St. Peter, St. Bartholomew, St. Edmund, St. Gregory, and St. Michael, and probably Walter Pope, vicar of All Saints, though we cannot be certain, as the date of institution of his successor, John Atte Brook, has been lost. The Master of St. John's Hospital and the Prioress of Delapre also fell victim to the disease, as did Robert Holcot, the eminent and learned Dominican Friar of Northampton, known as " the firm and unwearied doctor."

The effect of this terrible scourge was far-reaching in its social and economic aspects, but its saddest result was in connection with religion. The sudden removal of so large a proportion of the clerical body, left many a church, both in town and country, in dire straits. The bishops were compelled to institute young and uneducated clerics to the vacant livings, with often sad results in the way of ecclesiastical irregularities. The numbers and standing of those ordained and immediately instituted to benefices within the diocese of Lincoln, at the Christmas ordination of 1349, give a vivid idea of the terrible death rate among the clergy. At this ordination, which was held in the Carmelite church of St. Mary, at Stamford, seventy- six clerks were ordained to the diaconate, sixty as subdeacons, and thirteen as acolytes, and immediately instituted to livings! What must have been the condition of the " sacramentals " of all these parishes whose incumbents were only in minor orders?

Now you have an idea how the plague hit Northampton, but spare a thought to the everyday working men and women, wheelwrights, coopers, smithies, stonemasons, cooks, and vintners. So many trades lost skilled men and women. If building work was being carried out at the time of the plague, not only did the building take longer to complete, the skill level was seen to decrease markedly.

Our search through early documents soon led us to one particular person, Lord John Vintner/ Wynter, a knight, and his wife Joanna.

Their lands and tenements covered a wide area of Northamptonshire and beyond, and it is them, we believe from the documentation we have researched that the undercroft in George Row and the land on which it was built belonged.

This is what we know of his family line.

Henry Vinter/ Vyntner/Vynter
William Vinter had 3 sons - John, William & Almeric
John married Joanna, who died in 1357, with no children. Sir John Vynter, a distinguished knight, was knighted during the 34th year of the reign of Edward III.
William married Isabel and had 2 daughters - Alice and Agness
Almeric married Joan and had one son Henry
John Le Vinter Mayor 1341,1345, 1346, 1348, 1350 & 1351
Almeric Vinter Mayor 1366 & 1358
The Vinters were a prominent family in Northamptonshire during the 1300s and 1400s.
They held land and property in Northampton and also the Manor of Crick
The surname Vinter, Vyntner, Wynter, and Vynter are likely different spellings of the same family name, reflecting the occupation of wine merchants or vintners in medieval times.
This family line will help you while following the references below.

1357 This record is held by Northamptonshire Archives Service

Reference: A 81

Description:

Copy of enrolment on the Memoranda Rolls (31 Edw III) of the town of Northampton of the time of William Wakeleyn, mayor, provided by William Shifford, mayor and keeper of the common chest of the town.

Of the will of Johanna wife of Lord John Wynter, knight, dated Monday after Palm Sunday 1357. To be buried in St. James' monastery

To the abbot and convent a rent of 22s.8d. from a capital messuage and cellar on the west of the entrance thereof opposite the graveyard of All Saints Church and which Almeric Vynter and Joan his wife hold for life, and a rent of 10s. from a tenement which Alice once wife of John de Daylyngton holds for life in the Goldsmith's Street, and all the rents of those stalls which John de Brassyngburgh holds in the fish market, for 50 years with reversion on deaths of the lessees if they occur within the 50 years,

To the abbot and convent a croft in St.James's Street next one of Richard Smyth, and a shop in Cooks' now next one of William Pisford, and that shop in 'Spicers row which Peter de Ardern once held next a shop of the abbot and convent, and half of that room opposite 'le Potteschepyng' of Northampton town, and two empty stalls in the fish market opposite those of John de Brassyngburgh, for 50 years.

To the prior and convent of St. Andrew a tenement opposite All Saints Church on the south, next that which Henry Spicer holds, and two stalls which William Napton holds in butchers' row with another shop at the end of the row which William de Napton also holds opposite the stalls of the fishmongers, for 50 years. To the prioress and convent of a rent of 6s.2d. and a plot of land next a tenement once of John Trull on the north and Laurence Palmer's shop on the south, the rent issuing from a shop of Laurence Palmer in ironmongers' row, for 50 years, also a rent of 4s from that tenement which Henry Spicer holds and Matilda his wife opposite All Saints Church, and a rent of 13s. 4d. from a tenement John Colyn and Isabella his wife hold in mercers' row for their lives, and a rent of 12s.6d. from that shop which Elena Barbour holds in the row of the iron market for her life, - all for 50 years with reversion after death of lessees if sooner,

To the guardians of the fabric of St.Sepulchre's church a toft in the pig market next the highway on the east, and garden of William Reede on the west for 50 years. With remainder after 50 year terms of all above to the heirs and assigns of Lord John Vynter.

To Lord John her husband the capital messuage and a ploughland in Bedford that belonged to Beatrice her mother and all rents &c. inherited from Beatrice.

Executors Lord John her husband, and Lord Geoffrey, vicar of All Saints Church.

As we can see from these records, the Vynter family owned land and tenements all around All Saints Church and beyond. You will see as you read through the following files the family continued to be property owners and charge rent to various people and organisations. Disputes over rents and ownership also became part of daily life in medieval Northampton.

1360 -61 Ref: C 143/335/17

Held by: The National Archives, Kew, London.

John Vynter, knight, to grant messuages, land, and rent in Northampton, and the reversion of rent there charged on premises now held for life by Henry Spycer, Maud his wife, and John Colyn, to the prioress and nuns of Sewardsley, retaining land and rent in Crick, Northampton, Middleton, and Collingtree. N'hamp. Sewardsley Priory was a Priory occupied by Cistercian nuns in Showsley near Towcester, West Northamptonshire, England. The priory was established in the 12th century by a gift of Richard de Lestre during the reign of King Henry II.

1394 Reference: A 97
Date: Richard II
Held by: Northamptonshire Archives Services
Language: Latin
Description: Roll. Manor of Crek.
(Copy of assise of novel disseisin) Family dispute over land
Assizes held Friday before St.Peter in Cathedra 13 Richard II.

Henry Buckyngham v. Henry Vynter'.

H.V. recovered the land. Record of the case at assizes held at N'ton on Friday before St.Peter, in Cathedra 13 Richard II, States that the justices of the Common Bench had sent them the record of a novel disseisin at Westminster of Michaelmas term, 13 Richard II. Stating that the justices of the assize at Northampton had sent them a record of a case of novel disseisin, held before them at N'ton on the Friday before St.Peter in Cathedra, 12 Richard II. Whether Henry Buckyngham had disseised Henry Vynter of his freehold in Criek or of the manor of Criek called Vyntersmanere. Buckyngham appeared as a tenant of the manor and of an acre, parcel of the same, saying that Almeric Vynter of Northampton father of Henry, who is his heir, by his deed dated Sunday after St.Martin in Heme, 35 Edward III (1361), released to Thomas de Grantham and Alice his wife and the heirs of Alice who is the daughter of William cousin and heir of (Sir) John Vynter, knight, all rights in all land that had been, (Sir) John's in the town and fields of Northampton, Coton, Criek, Lilleburne or elsewhere in Northants. Buckyngham now held Thomas and Alice's estate therein (?).

The deed was inrolled in the presence of de Geydyngton, mayor of the town, and of Thomas Elys and Laurence Haddon bailiffs in the hustings held on Monday after St.Andrew Apostle 35 Edward III (1361).

Henry Vynter however disagrees stating that William Vynter had 3 sons: John, William and Almeric and that in Easter term 16 Edward (III, 1342) he levied a fine of the manor of Crek to his son John and John's wife Joan and their issue with reversion in default of issue to himself; that he died and then Joan died without issue.

William the 2nd son married at Pensehurst in Kent Isabella Coubill (?) and had 2 daughters, Alice and Agnes and then John died whereupon the property devolved on Alice and Agnes whose estate was now in Buckyngham. Henry Vynter as son and heir of Almeric claimed as cousin and heir of John saying the daughters were illegitimate.

Henry said the acre was not geldable but was without the liberties of Northampton and that Almeric whilst at Charyngcros was seized by Henry Buckyngham and 14 others and forced to execute the deed mentioned.

Buckyngham however replied that Almeric was a burgess of Northampton at the time and, that at that time Thomas Grantham and Alice were seised of a messuage in Kyngeswelle street and other tenements in N'ton, his estate in which Almeric released by the deed records the progress of the case through the courts until its trial by a named jury at N'ton in the custody of Ralph Parles the sheriff to whom a certain John Howel, armsbearer of Lord Ralph Basset came with further evidence on behalf of the plaintiff and Henry son of Henry Buckyngham on behalf of the defendant. John produced a charter of the entail of the manor on the ancestors of Henry Vynter.

The case was retried before another jury and subsequently in response to a writ dated 23 Oct. 18 (Ri II, 1394) judgment was given that Henry Vynter recover his seisin of the manor.

30th September 1399, Reference: C 131/224/32
Held by: The National Archives, Kew, London.
Description: Debtor: Robert Archer, citizen, and mercer of Winchester
Creditor: Richard Harpour, citizen
Before whom: Mayor of the Staple of Westminster.
Sent by: Chancery.
Endorsement: The writ was sent to the bailiffs of the town of Northampton.
Note: Inquisition and return: Date to be returned: The bailiffs of the liberty of Northampton said that Robert had on the day of the recognisance within the liberty a tenement called the Blackhall .... in the Sweynwell of the town of Northampton, four cottages with gardens in the Cowland, and a tenement in the Spicery opposite the church of All Saints (Both ends of the document are torn away and much is illegible)

1410 Robert Archer Reference: C 241/202/41
Held by: The National Archives, Kew, London.
Debtor: Robert Archer, a citizen, and mercer of Winchester [a city in Hants.].
Creditor: Richard Harper {Harpour}, a citizen and mercer of London.
Amount: £400.
Before whom: Richard Whittington, Mayor of the Westminster Staple [Middx].
When taken: 31/08/1410
First term: 25/12/1410
Last term: 25/12/1410
Writ to: Sheriff of Northants
Sent by: Chancery.
Endorsement: Matthew Swettenham {Swetenham}, Sheriff [of Northants.], replies that he sent the writ to Nicholas Hilton and John Derby, Bailiffs of the Liberty of the Town of Northampton, who replied as appears in the extent.

Note: Inquisition and return: Date given for the return to Chancery: 13/10/1412. Attached is the extent made on Fri., 09/09/1412, before Nicholas Hilton and John Derby, Bailiffs of the Liberty of Northampton. Robert Archer had on the day of the recognisance in fee simple a tenement, called Blake Hall {le Blakehalle}, with three cottages annexed in Swinewell Street {le Swynwelstrete} in the Town of Northampton, and 4 cottages with adjacent gardens in Cow Lane {le Cowelane} in Northampton, and a tenement in Spicers' Row opposite the Church of All Saints in Northampton; he held on the day of the recognisance, and afterwards, a tenement next to the aforesaid tenement in Spicers' Row, from the Prior and Convent of St Andrew, Northampton, for the term of 100 years and more; altogether the property is worth 8m. after expenses. He has no other lands or tenements, goods, or chattels.

1414-15: John Spring Mayor

1416 Edmund Ferrers
Reference: C 131/59/10
Held by: The National Archives, Kew, London.
Description: Debtor: Edmund Ferrers, of Northampton [a borough in Hamfordshoe Hundred] in Northants.
Before whom: Writ to: Sheriff of [Northants.]
Sent by: Chancery.
Note: Inquisition and return: Date given for the return to Chancery: Only the extent survives. It was made on Fri., 24/01/1416, before Thomas Sale and John Spriggy, Bailiffs of the Liberty of the Town of Northampton [a borough in Hamfordshoe Hundred]. Edmund had a close, called Latimer's Croft {Latymerscroft}, lying in Knights Street {le knyghtstrete} of the Town of Northampton, and a croft lying outside the East Gate of Northampton, which are worth 23s. 4d. Edmund held on the day of the recognisance, and afterwards, for the

term of his wife Alice's life, who was formerly the wife of Henry Vintner {Vynter}, a tenement, called The Back Hand {le Bakhond}, situated opposite the Church of All Saints in Spicers' Row {le Spicersrow} in the Town of Northampton, and two shops situated in the Butchers' Ring {in Rengo [!] Carnificum} of Northampton, and three fish-stalls situated in the market of the town; two shops situated in The Malt-Row {le Maltrow} of the town, which Thomas Crosse holds at will for 6s. 8d.; and an annual rent from a shop which John Woodward holds in the market: together they are worth 66s. Edmund held on the day of the recognisance, and afterwards, for the term of his wife Alice's life, and for four years after her decease, a tenement in Abingdon {le Abyndon} Street in Northampton for a term of 60 years by the grant of Isolda Ward, which is worth 13s. 4d. after expenses. He has no other lands or tenements, goods or chattels in the Liberty of Northampton.

1418 Henry Vinter Reference: C 131/60/7
Held by: The National Archives, Kew, London.
Legal status: Public Record(s)
Language: English
He held 2 tenements in Spicers Row, but lost them to the crown. Debtor: Henry Vintner {Vynter}, of Northampton [a borough in Northants.].
Creditor: John Leir {Leyre}, and John Grant {Graunt}, clerks, now deceased, and John Brown, clerk.
Amount: £300.
Before whom: Nicholas Exton, Mayor of the Westminster Staple [Middx].
When taken: 11/07/1390
First term: 25/12/1390
Last term: 25/12/1390

Writ to: Sheriff of Northants
Sent by: Chancery.

Endorsement: John Mansel {Mauncell}, Sheriff [of Northants.], replies that he has extended all the lands and tenements of Henry Vintner {Vynter} outside the Liberty of Northampton and seized them into the King's hands; he sent the writ to the Bailiffs of Northampton, and they replied as appears in the schedule.

Note: Inquisition and return: Date given for the return to Chancery: 03/11/1418. Attached is: (a) The extent of his lands and tenements in Northants. outside the Liberty of Northampton made at Daventry [in Fawsley Hundred] before John Mansel, Sheriff [of Northants.], on Wed., 02/11/1418: Henry had on the day of the recognisance the Manor of Creek, worth £20 after expenses. (b) The extent made at Northampton before John Barnhill and William Perry {Piry}, Bailiffs of the Town, on Sat., 29/10/1418 [the jury include a mercer, a fuller, and a glasier]. Henry Vinter had a tenement in Spicers' Row in Northampton, called Back House {Bakhous}, situated between a draper's tenement and the shop of John Snell, mercer, and it has a long entrance {habet longum introitum}; it is worth 20s. after expenses. He has another tenement in Spicers' Row, which has a long entrance and is worth 20s. after expenses; and two shops in the Malt Row of Northampton, which an ironmonger holds, worth 13s. 4d. after expenses. Also, he has two shops in the Butchery, which two butchers hold, worth 20s. after expenses; and three stalls in the Market, worth 3s. after expenses; and an annual rent of 6s. 8d. from a shop, with chambers above it, which a mercer holds in the Mercers' Row of Northampton. He has no other goods, or chattels, lands, or tenements in Northampton. Dorse: memorandum that on 01/11/1418 the manor, tenements, shops, and rents were delivered to John Brown.

1430-31: William Rushden (MP for Northampton, 1411) Mayor

1432-1443, possibly 1467-1470 Richard Fyssh. John Pyry
Reference: C 1/11/532
Held by: The National Archives, Kew
Short title: Fyssh v Pyry.
Subject:
Lease of `a place called the Tabard' in Northampton; false imprisonment, etc. Northamptonshire

1504 The condition of the town of Northampton in 1504 is shown by a rental in which the town is divided into streets with the lanes running off on either side into market rows and districts. Probably the most important area was 'Swinwel-strete,' now Derngate, which was apparently the residential quarter, and included the manor of Gobions and the Grange. The latter, which formerly belonged to Thomas Latimer, was late of Thomas Tresham, and then held by John Chauncy. It included land next the postern called Derngate and other adjoining land. Property here belonged to the chapel of Blessed Mary the Virgin in All Saints Church, and to the fraternity of Holy Trinity. There were inns called 'le Crown,' 'le Bell,' 'le Tabard,' and 'le Bulle,' and a house called 'le Blakhall.'
St. Giles Street, which extended to the town wall, was mostly inhabited by tradesmen, bakers and fullers and Adam 'le Garlikemonger.' In Abingdon (Habyngdon) Street, leading to the East Gate, was a quarry.

Le Tabard, the hospice situated opposite All Saints' Church in Northampton, holds historical significance. In the past, it was frequented by travellers and pilgrims. The name itself evokes images of weary wayfarers seeking rest and sustenance. The hospice, like a silent witness, stood witness to the ebb and flow of lives passing through its doors. Whether sheltering weary knights or humble traders, the cellars of Le Tabard remain a fragment of history and a hidden jewel of Northampton's history.

1532
Held by: Northamptonshire Archives Service
Reference: FH1139
Date: 10 Aug 24 Henry VIII [1532]
Language: Latin
Description: Grant Thomas Tresham, Kt.

To Edward Mountagu, serjeant at law, Ralph Fremane, merchant of the staple, and others, dwelling in Northampton by the Bell on East, Cappe Lane on South, All Saints cemetery on North.

1675

The great fire of Northampton consumed a huge part of the town and the area we are concerned with did not escape. All Saints church was destroyed, all but the tower.

At this point, it is important to mention that a discovery was made to the south of All Saints Church of a medieval two light plate tracery window in the west wall of, what is now, the Whitworth Chambers. This window is thought to be in-situ and dates from the 14th century, interestingly the same date as the county Club Cellars. It is possible that there was a stone building above the cellars, built at the same time.

For more information regarding the window please read The County Club Report, Survey Notes 18th August 2003 by Brian L Giggins MA, MCIfA.

Conclusions

We started this research to see if early information about the medieval cellars in George Row could be found. We had two questions, who owned the land, and why was it built?

We have found out who initially owned the land. As we have mentioned previously, during the Norman conquest, William systematically dispossessed English landowners and conferred their property on his continental followers. Simon de St. Liz (Senlis), accompanied William "the Conqueror" to England. He was created Earl of Huntingdon and Northampton in [1087/90]. He then divided the land up gifting it to Knights of the realm.

What we have not found is concrete evidence that the cellars were built as an ecclesiastical building. Many of the properties on le Spicerow were once owned by the wealthy Vinter/ Vyntner family. One property was gifted by the family to The Prior and Convent of St Andrews and money from this tenement, and others went straight to the church.

John Chauncy owned land next the postern called Derngate and other adjoining land. Property here belonged to the chapel of Blessed Mary the Virgin in All Saints Church, and to the fraternity of Holy Trinity. There were inns called 'le Crown,' 'le Bell,' 'le Tabard,' and 'le Bulle,' and a house called 'le Blakhall.' These inns were in existence at the same time, some in 'Swinwel-street, and some in le Spicerow.

We are left with questions still to be answered.

1 If we think the cellars were built in the 14th century, what was the building above the cellar used for in the first 100 years of its life?

2 Could it have been a wealthy wine merchant's house, (Vinter, Vyntner, Wynter, and Vynter) before becoming Le Tabard in 1433?

3 As this cellar is one of the oldest existing parts of medieval Northampton, why has there, to my knowledge, never been an extensive archaeological study done down there?

We would have loved to spend more time researching the Northampton and County Club Cellars; however, time and other pending projects were not on our side.

This book has been compiled to give the next researchers, whoever they may be, reference points to begin their research. I hope in time to come, these mid-14th century cellars, hidden jewels of Northampton's past, will be promoted with pride. It is one piece of Northampton's heritage that deserves to be protected for future generations.

Adrian H Perkins